メエハ

Why do people join Gangs?

Julie Johnson

RAINTREE
STECK-VAUGHN
PUBLISHERS

A Harcourt Company

Austin New York
www.steck-vaughn.com

Published by Raintree Steck-Vaughn Publishers, an imprint of Steck-Vaughn Company

Library of Congress Cataloging-in-Publication Data
Johnson, Julie.
Why do people join gangs / Julie Johnson.
    p.   cm.—(Exploring tough issues)
    Includes bibliographical references and index.
    ISBN 0-7398-3236-0
    1. Gangs—Juvenile literature. [1. Gangs.]
    I. Title. II. Series.

Printed in Italy. Bound in the United States.
1 2 3 4 5 6 7 8 9 0 05 04 03 02 01

Picture acknowledgments
The publisher would like to thank the following for their kind permission to use their pictures:

AFP 29; Associated Press 6/Tribune Star, 8, 13/Macau Jornar Va Kio, 25/Springfield Union News, 43; Camera Press 11/Adrian Sutton; Chapel Studios *title page* & 5/Tim Garrod, Eye Ubiquitous *cover* & 34; Sally and Richard Greenhill 31; Angela Hampton Family Picture Library 35, 36, 38, 39, 41, 45; Hodder Wayland Picture Library *contents page* (right)/Tizzie Knowles, 18/Chris Schwarz, 27/Tizzie Knowles, 30/Martyn Chillmaid, 32/Chris Fairclough, 37/Martyn Chillmaid, 40/Chris Fairclough; Photofusion 33/Paul Baldesare; Pictorial Press *contents page* (bottom), 13, 16, 20/Jeffrey Mayer; Panos 9/Philip Wolmuth; Popperfoto 42; Popperfoto/Reuters 14, 15, 17, 22, 23, 26, 28, 44; Tony Stone 7/David Young-Wolff; Unicorn 4, 10, 19, 21, 24.

Contents

1. What is a gang?

What do you think a gang is?

What picture comes into your mind when you think of a gang? The group of friends you hang out with on weekends? Or a rowdy crowd of thugs? People have different ideas about what a gang is. You can read the views of some young people on the right.

> A gang is…
> "A group of people who go around together and have a good time."
> "A group of people who are sometimes mean to other people."
> *Thoughts from two 9-year-olds*
>
> "A group of people who cause trouble."
> "A group of people who aim to look out for each other's needs."
> *Thoughts from two 15-year-old boys*

When you look up the word "gang" in a dictionary it says a gang is a group of people who get together, sometimes to carry out a criminal activity or behave in an anti-social way. A gang can be small—as few as three or four people—or it can involve many people.

◀ *Most gangs are made up of young men but there are some mixed and some all-girl gangs. These girls belong to an American gang called the Basset Grande.*

Young people sometimes talk about having a "gang of friends" but being part of a real gang is different than just hanging out with a few people. Gang members are usually linked closely together in some way. Like a sports team, they might all wear the same clothes. Often they share a common identity, usually through a gang name. They might also develop their own language, signs, and symbols. This gives them a stronger sense of being part of a group. It also means that other people can recognize them as members of a gang.

Some of the most serious international crime is carried out by gangs, but a gang can also be a group of people going along to watch their favorite football team. In this book, we will look mainly at gangs who bully, intimidate, and commit crime.

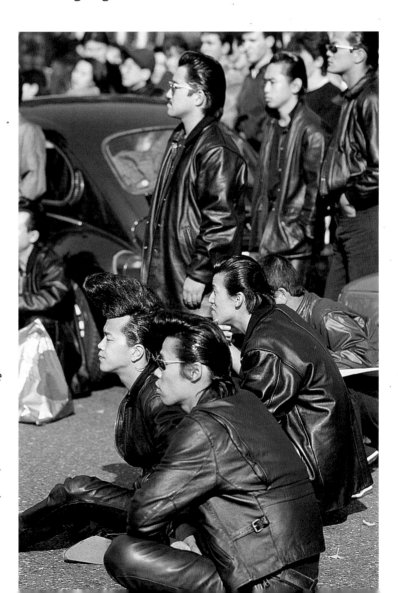

▶ The "Bamboo Tribe" is a Japanese gang. Its members are linked by their interest in rock and roll music. Like the American rock and roll stars of the 1950s, they all wear leather bikers' jackets and have slicked-back hair.

Rites and rituals

Gangs often have what are called rites or rituals. Initiation rites are things people have to do before they are accepted as gang members. For instance, they might have to make a pledge to be loyal to the rest of the gang and then prove their loyalty in some way.

Rites can be harmless fun. But they can also be dangerous and frightening. In initiation rites for some street gangs, there is an "interview" where the person wanting to join the gang (the "candidate") boasts of the tough, hard things he or she has done. The other gang members may then beat the candidate up to test his or her toughness.

▲ *The Ku Klux Klan is a racist organization in the United States. Small gangs of Klan members, wearing hoods and white robes, hold rituals in which they burn a cross.*

Some gangs expect their members to do things that are dangerous, violent, or against the law. They might insist that a new member harms someone, possibly from a rival gang, before he or she can join their gang. Others might dare a new member to run across a busy street or steal something from a store, to prove they really want to be part of the gang. This is a way of testing how loyal the person will be to the gang in the future.

▶ Daring a new gang member to shoplift things from a store is a way of testing her loyalty.

case study · case study · case study · case study · case study

Paulo's gang has several different rituals that all new gang members have to go through before they can be accepted. First, they have to cross train tracks when a train is coming. This is to show their courage and prove that the gang is important to them. That is not enough, though. To prove their strength and ability to stand up for themselves, they have to pick a fight with a boy in the gang or from another gang—and win.

Gang identity

In street gangs all over the world, gangs use different ways to identify themselves and mark out their territory—or "turf."

Each gang has special hand signs that identify its own members. Fights between gangs can often start when members of different gangs flash their hand signals at each other.

> "We like to wear clothes with the Los Angeles Raiders' logo on them because it tells other gangs that we are tough and not to be messed with."
>
> *Danny, age 15*

The members of a gang might all wear clothes of the same color, or they might all wear a similar item of clothing or jewelry. It could be a particular type of hat worn in a specific way, a pendant, or a ring. Five or six-pointed jewelry is common among gang members. They might even all have the same unusual haircut. A gang member who chooses not to wear the "uniform" of the gang risks getting beaten up.

▶ *Members of neo-Nazi gangs often have "skinhead" haircuts that make them look tough.*

Members of street gangs often have tattoos to show that they belong to a particular gang and to warn off rival gangs. Some tattoos have special meanings—for example, a spider's web shows that the wearer has spent time in prison.

In areas where gangs hang out, walls and buildings are often covered with brightly colored signs and pictures. This is called graffiti. The word "graffiti" comes from an Italian word meaning "inscription." There are plenty of graffiti artists who are not gang members at all: they just love to paint graffiti. However, gangs do use graffiti as a way of marking out their territory, communicating messages, throwing down challenges, and posting triumphs. It's a bit like a bulletin board on the Internet. Graffiti can sometimes be used to remember a gang member who has died. Painting over a rival gang's graffiti is seen as a challenge to fight.

▶ The hand signs these men are making show that they are members of the Diamond Street gang in Los Angeles, California. The gang's graffiti is on the wall behind them.

2. Street gangs

What is a street gang?

In many towns and cities around the world, you will find young people who belong to street gangs. Research carried out in the United States shows that street gangs often form in cities where there are a lot of young people.

> "They are dying to die..."
> *An American priest, speaking about gang members in Los Angeles, California*

These gangs are often involved in crime, especially theft and drug-dealing. One gang might be the most powerful group in a particular housing project or neighborhood. Other people who live in the area may be afraid to challenge them or report them to the police if they break the law.

In the United States, four of the main gangs are the Crips and the Bloods, based in Los Angeles, and the Folk Nation and the People Nation, based in Chicago. There are many smaller gangs, too, in these and other cities.

▼ *Members of the Tiny Locos gang show off their many tattoos.*

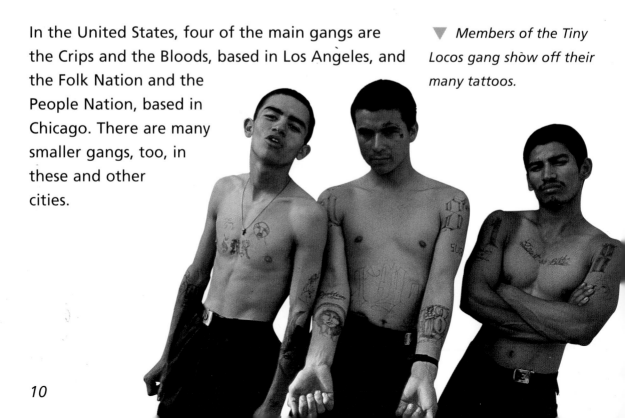

Some young people in Russia have divided into two main gangs who often fight each other. They are the "Skins," a neo-Nazi gang who are violently racist, and the "Rappers," who are similar to the rap-loving gangs found in American cities. Just off Red Square, in the middle of Moscow, the Russian capital these two armies of Russian youth often come face to face.

These masked men are members of the Crips gang.

> "I will fight for my entire life for the right to wear trousers that hang down to my knees. We live only for ourselves. We devote all our time to break-dancing, graffiti, and rap music."
>
> *Denis, a 17-year-old Russian "Rapper"*

FACT:
In Los Angeles alone, there are more than 400 gangs with 65,000 members. More than one person dies every day as a result of warfare between gangs.
BBC *Today* program, June 2000

Criminal gangs

Some of the biggest and best-known criminal gangs are the Mafia in the United States, the Cosa Nostra in Italy, the Yazuka in Japan, the Triads in Southeast Asia, and the Yardies from the Caribbean.

The Triads operate throughout Southeast Asia. Triad gangs have names like Sung Lion and Four Seas. These names may sound romantic but the gangs are actually responsible for running large crime syndicates. They have a lot of power in such places such as Taiwan and Shanghai in China.

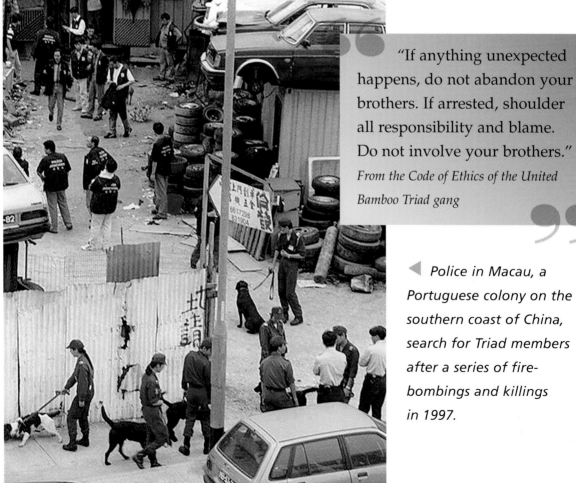

"If anything unexpected happens, do not abandon your brothers. If arrested, shoulder all responsibility and blame. Do not involve your brothers."
From the Code of Ethics of the United Bamboo Triad gang

◀ Police in Macau, a Portuguese colony on the southern coast of China, search for Triad members after a series of fire-bombings and killings in 1997.

▶ *A scene from* The Godfather, *a film starring Marlon Brando (third from left), that showed the power of the Mafia in organized crime.*

The name "Yardies" is given to criminals from the poor backyards of Kingston, Jamaica. In recent years, groups of British-born young black men have begun to copy the Yardies, attracted by their "glamorous" gun-toting image. There are thought to be about 80 to 200 Yardies in Great Britain. The police do not officially acknowledge that they exist, but in one month alone the Yardies were thought to have carried out eight murders of other black people in London.

"*The killings are worn as a badge of honor.*"
A police officer who investigated the Yardies' involvement in violent crime.

The Mafia is perhaps the most famous gang of all. The gang formed in Sicily many years ago and has spread to other parts of the world, especially the rest of Italy and the United States. The Mafia was the subject of a series of movies called *The Godfather*. The films showed how a big gang was organized, how it demanded loyalty, and how ruthless it could be with anyone who went against its interests.

Drug dealing and protection rackets

These Colombian police officers are inspecting a sack of marijuana. On this occasion, officers seized more than 17 tons of the illegal drug, which was being secretly shipped to Italy.

Since the 1980s, the use of illegal drugs has increased. Gangs control the international trade in drugs, worth millions of pounds. For example, a local gang in the Far East might oversee the growing of plants that are used to make heroin. The drugs are sold in large quantities to bigger gangs that arrange for them to be smuggled to Europe and the United States. Once there, the drugs are sold again in smaller and smaller quantities until the drugs reach a local street gang selling to users in their area. In some countries, such as Colombia, there is extreme violence between rival drug cartels as each struggles for a bigger share of the drug trade.

FACT:
42 percent of youth gangs in the United States were involved in the street sale of drugs in order to make money for the gang.
1997 National Youth Gangs Survey

Drugs are not the only goods that are traded illegally by gangs. Whenever the sale of something is restricted or forbidden, gangs move in. So, for example, if there is an international ban on arms sales to a particular country, gangs get involved in supplying arms illegally.

Gangs such as the Triads also operate protection rackets. They force the owners of businesses to pay money to them in exchange for protection from other gangs. Business owners who refuse to pay or do not have enough money may be beaten up by the gang. Their stores or restaurants may be damaged.

In some countries, gangs are so powerful that they can even interfere with the running of the country. They bribe government officials, judges, and police officers, or threaten them so that they will not interfere with the gangs' activities. One country that is particularly badly affected in this way is Russia.

▼ *Police officers in Moscow, Russia, arrest members of a local mafia gang.*

Are gangs new?

Gangs are not new. Stories from ancient Greek and Roman times describe groups of young men ambushing other young men and beating up their victims. Shakespeare's play *Romeo and Juliet*, written in the 1590s, tells the story of two feuding families, the Capulets and the Montagues. A film version of this story, made in 1997 and starring Leonardo di Caprio, shows them as modern gangs in late twentieth-century Verona Beach, Florida.

▼ *The Capulet gang prepares to take on the Montagues, in this scene from the 1997 film version of* Romeo and Juliet.

The earliest American gangs, with names like the Fly Boys, were recorded at the end of the eighteenth century. In the nineteenth century, Irish immigrants formed gangs. One, the Forty Thieves, had dress codes and a strong leader, and they called their members by nicknames. As more and more immigrants came to live in the United States, gang membership grew.

By the 1920s, there were 1,313 gangs in Chicago, with more than 25,000 members. By the 1940s, Chicano (Mexican-American) gangs ruled the streets of Los Angeles. They were easily identified by their "zoot suits"—tapered trousers and long, wide-shouldered jackets, worn with broad-brimmed hats.

FACT:
1980: 2,000 gangs; 100,000 gang members
1996: 31,000 gangs; 846,000 gang members
Studies of gangs in the United States by Miller
(1992) and Moore and Terrett (2000).

In 1948, a famous motorcycle gang called Hell's Angels was founded in San Bernardino, California. Hell's Angels belong to groups called "chapters." Today, there are more than 70 Hell's Angels chapters in Europe and the United States, as well as chapters in Australia, New Zealand, and South Africa.

Gang violence was severe in the United States in the 1950s. New York gangs—African-American, white, Puerto Rican—fought over "turf" (territory) and girls. Words like "jitterbugging"—meaning "to fight"—became well known even outside the gangs.

▼ These bikers are members of a South African chapter of the Hell's Angels.

Since the 1980s, the number of youth gangs in the United States has increased dramatically. It has become easier to get hold of guns, so the gangs have become more violent. More guns, combined with an increase in the number of gang members owning cars, has led to an increase in the number of drive-by shootings.

3. Why do people join gangs?

Family or friends?

FACT:
Research done in the United States showed that the peak age for being in a gang was 17, although gang members ranged from 12-25 years of age.
Studies by Miller (1982) and Spergel (1991)

We all like to feel we belong somewhere—to be part of a group. Joining a gang can be a normal part of growing up. When we are very young, our families are more important to us than our friends. As we get older and move into our teenage years, our friends and peers become more important. This is the age when young people are most likely to become members of a gang.

► *For most young people, hanging out with friends is a harmless way of spending time.*

For some, joining a gang can be a way of rebelling against their family, especially if the gang is involved in activities they know their parents would not like. Other young people join gangs because there are problems in their family lives. For example, their parents may have broken up, or they may have been placed with several sets of foster parents, or brought up in an orphange. Being in the gang gives them a feeling of security that they cannot find elsewhere.

In some communities, young people find that their families expect them to become gang members. In Italy and the United States, for example, Mafia gangs are often made up of several members of one family. As the boys in the family grow up they are expected to join the gang, too.

▼ *For some young people, gangs provide closer relationships than their own families.*

Why do people join street gangs?

Young people join street gangs for many different reasons. The music and lyrics of rap, and certain movies, can glamorize gang life. They make joining a gang seem the cool thing to do. Pressure from friends to join a gang can be hard to resist. In areas where there are many gangs, it can seem safer to join one and have the protection of other gang members.

> "We had a gang ... where I grew up—we felt part of something and had good fun together. Didn't really do anything wrong except knock on people's doors and run away. Things like that."
>
> *Gentleman, age 60*

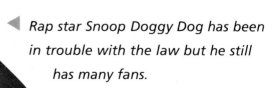

Rap star Snoop Doggy Dog has been in trouble with the law but he still has many fans.

Young people also join street gangs for these reasons:
• They are poor and think that joining a gang is an easy way to make money fast. Often, gang members drive around in big cars paid for with the money they make from crime, mostly drug dealing.
• They are unemployed; being an active gang member is a way to stay busy and occupied.
• They are discriminated against: many people from ethnic minorities join gangs for a sense of security and togetherness.
• They live in poor, run-down parts of cities from which there seems to be no escape. Belonging to a gang can offer excitement and adventure in lives that are otherwise full of boredom and despair.

▲ *Owning a big car is an important status symbol for many young gang members.*

FACT:
80 percent of street gang members in the United States have poor literacy skills and cannot read or write well.
alphabase.com/website/gangs

Outsiders

People sometimes join gangs because they feel threatened. For example, in any school or neighborhood there are usually a few people who are seen as different in some way. Often, they are bullied or left out by their peers. They sometimes get together with other people who are in the same situation and form their own gang for protection. Occasionally, gangs like this develop a hatred of the people who have treated them badly.

▼ *Students at Columbine High School write messages on the coffin of one of the girls killed in the shootings.*

FACT:
In 1999, Eric Harris and Dylan Klebold shot and killed several students and teachers at Columbine High School in Colorado, and then killed themselves. The two boys were members of a school gang, known as the "Trenchcoat Mafia" because of the coats they all wore. One of the other gang members told a CNN interviewer that the gang had been teased by other students. This may have played a part in triggering the murders.

24

Young neo-Nazis on the march in Germany. Gangs there have carried out attacks on immigrants.

People who belong to an ethnic minority sometimes feel unwelcome or out of place. By forming a gang with other members of their ethnic group, they may feel they are less likely to be attacked.

Some people join gangs because they feel their way of life is under threat. Gangs of racists sometimes claim that they feel their country is being "swamped" by people from different ethnic backgrounds. Often the people who join such gangs are poorly educated or live in areas of high unemployment. They see themselves as having to compete with people from different cultures for jobs or better homes and are afraid that they will lose out.

4. The trouble with gangs...

Gang mentality

When young people join gangs they sometimes begin to do things that they would never do if they were on their own. This is sometimes described as developing a "gang mentality." They get drawn into crime or other dangerous activities such as substance abuse.

The first time a gang steals a car or sprays graffiti on a wall, it seems really daring. The gang members egg each other on, making themselves feel braver. Some might not want to get involved, but they dare not say so for fear of being laughed at. They may get a real sense of excitement from doing something they are not supposed to do. It can be almost like taking a drug, making them feel "high." They want to do it again—and next time it seems much easier.

▶ Graffiti-covered buildings are a common sight in gangland, making urban areas look more run-down and threatening.

To keep getting a kick from their activities, gangs sometimes find they need to take greater and greater risks. For example, they begin by vandalizing cars, move on to stealing car radios, and perhaps eventually steal cars and start joyriding. As they are in a group, they feel there is less chance that they will be identified and caught.

For the gang members, activities like these are "just a laugh," but the results can be serious. In their local area they get a reputation as troublemakers. If they are involved in dangerous activities they might be injured, or even killed. They might get involved with bigger gangs of older people who carry out more serious crimes such as drug-dealing, robberies, and shootings. Some will get caught by the police. Mass arrests of gang members regularly take place, as police try to control their activities.

▲ This picture shows the man believed to be the leader of the Latin Kings gang in Massachusetts, appearing in court in 1998.

"I never thought I would end up in prison. It all started with stealing things from the local shop next to school when I was nine."
Graham, age 20

Gang addicts

Sometimes gang members become involved in substance abuse. This might include sniffing glue or aerosol sprays or using illegal drugs such as marijuana, cocaine, or heroin. Gangs tend to form in areas where there is poverty and high unemployment. Often, drugs are easily available in such areas. Many gangs deal in drugs as well as using them.

▼ This homeless boy belongs to a street gang in Manila in the Philippines. He is sniffing glue.

At first substance abuse can seem exciting. The drug or other substance makes users feel high. Being part of a gang that is not afraid to take risks gives them a kick, too. They might enjoy the thrill of taking part in a secret activity that is shared only with other gang members.

case study · case study · case study · case study · case study

"I was brought up in a housing project where drugs were just part of life. Everyone was using them, and when I joined the gang it just seemed the right thing to do. It all started with sniffing glue and then I got into cannabis. After that I got caught stealing some things from a local store. I was planning to sell the stuff and use the money to buy cannabis. It just went on from there. I couldn't get out of the gang—I owed one of them money for drugs and he just kept making me steal more and more things."

Steve, age 16

As Steve found out, the problem with substance abuse is that it is not always easy to stop. People can find themselves becoming addicted, and their health may be damaged. Drug addicts often have to steal the money they need to buy more drugs. They are addicted to an activity they carry out as part of a gang, so they may find it very difficult to leave the gang even if they want to.

▶ *Drug dealing is an important way for a gang to earn money. Drug users who fail to pay for the drugs they use may be beaten up.*

Gangs and violence

People often link gangs with violence, although not all gangs are violent. Gangs attract people who want to appear tough. They are eager to prove how tough they are to themselves and other gang members. They might challenge people within their own gang to a fight or attack members of other gangs.

Some people get a kick out of violence, in the same way that some people get a kick out of taking drugs or stealing cars. Because they are part of a gang, they feel a great sense of power over other people. Gangs sometimes target specific groups, perhaps people from another school or people from a different ethnic group.

▼ *British teenager Stephen Lawrence was murdered by a racist gang in 1994. His parents (shown here) complained that the police did not investigate the murder properly.*

Street gangs sometimes become involved in "turf wars" as each gang tries to protect its territory from rivals. Often gangs are involved in some illegal activity, such as supplying drugs to users in their area. They make a lot of money from doing this. If other gangs move in and try to take over, the local gang has to fight to protect its income. Turf wars can become extremely violent.

◀ *A police officer checks a suspected gang member for weapons.*

FACT:
An estimated 3,340 gang members were murdered by other gang members in the United States in 1997.
1997 National Youth Gangs Survey

case study · case study · case study · case study · case study

Mario, 17, lives in an inner-city neighborhood. One day a gang from another neighborhood showed up. They walked around as if they owned the place. The local boys felt angry. Eventually, they organized themselves into a gang. They wanted to protect their territory from the invaders. There was some fighting, but it stopped when some older boys brought both gangs together to sit down and talk about it. The other gang left. Mario and his friends did not have any more problems and have disbanded their gang as they feel they do not need it any longer.

5. Gangs and bullying

School gangs

Gangs can be found in all types of schools. Like most adults, children want to feel that other people like them. Being accepted by a gang is a way of proving to themselves and other people that they are "all right."

When 11-year-old Max started his new school, there was a group of boys who called themselves "The Boys." Everyone seemed to want to be part of this gang. Max had been bullied at his old school, and his dad had told him to get in with the big boys to keep it from happening again. Max just wanted to make some friends; he didn't really want to be part of a gang. One of the gang members lived on the same street as Max and he seemed friendly. Max decided to hang around with him, and eventually he got into the gang. No one picked on him when he was with the gang, and his dad was really pleased that at last he had some friends. The only problem was that Max had no real friends outside the gang.

◀ *Lonely children are sometimes only too glad to join a gang.*

There are different types of school gangs. Some are tough gangs—perhaps the biggest boys or girls in the school, who are eager to prove just how tough they are. They might have older brothers or sisters who belong to street gangs, or they might be street gang members themselves. Some are trendy gangs whose members know all about the latest music and electronic games, and all have mobile phones. Other gangs are gangs of bullies.

Children outside the gang may feel intimidated, or they may wish that they were more like the gang. Areas of the school may become "no-go areas," where only gang members hang out.

▼ *Gangs of boys like this can be intimidating to other children, even if the boys are just getting together for a ball game.*

What is bullying?

It is quite common for school gangs to be involved in bullying. Bullies rarely work on their own. Being part of a gang makes them feel more secure and powerful.

Bullying is when one person or a group of people deliberately set out to hurt another person, either physically or mentally. Bullying can take many different forms, as the quotes on these pages show. There is an old saying that "Sticks and stones may break my bones but words can never hurt me." In fact, teasing and making cruel comments can be just as damaging as physical bullying.

"She doesn't touch me or hit me. It's just the way she looks at me and says 'I'll get you.' Mother says she's just showing off, but one day I think she will get me."

Lisa, age 11

▼ *Forcing other pupils to hand over food, money, or other valuable possessions is a favorite pastime for bullies.*

Some people still believe that bullying doesn't do people any real harm. They might tell victims of bullying to stand up for themselves or to hit back. They might even say that being bullied makes the victim mentally stronger in the long run. But bullying can make people feel too powerless to stand up for themselves, while hitting back can sometimes get the victim into trouble. Some people have become so depressed by bullying that they have committed suicide. In the last twenty years, schools and parents have started to realize how damaging bullying can be.

▲ *Gangs of bullies often lie in wait for their victims in quiet areas where no one else will see what is going on.*

"They push and shove me, or trip me whenever we pass in school."
Paul, age 12

Why do some people bully?

People join gangs of bullies for many different reasons. Some children find it difficult to get along with others. They may come from homes where their parents are very aggressive towards them and each other. They have not been taught how to work things out with other people.

Other children may have been spoiled at home—not corrected when they do things that are wrong or given anything they want when they want it. They might not have been encouraged to consider and care about other people's feelings.

▼ *Some children join gangs of bullies because they see threats and fighting as the only way to get what they want.*

case study · case study · case study · case study · case study

Marsha, age 12, knew things were not good between her mother and father. They were always shouting at each other. Her dad came home from work later and later, and then suddenly he just left. No one really talked to Marsha about what was going on. She was angry and confused.

That was when she got into a gang at school and started bullying other children. The school contacted her mother, who was really upset with Marsha, saying she had enough to deal with already. Marsha felt no one seemed to be thinking about how she felt. The bullying was just a way of letting her feelings out—at least it meant that someone took some notice of her.

Some people bully because they have been bullied themselves and decide the best way to stop it is to begin to bully others. Or there may have been big changes at home that they are finding it difficult to cope with, such as a new baby, a death in the family, or their parents splitting up. They feel left out, angry, and upset. Bullying becomes a way of drawing attention to themselves and how they are feeling.

▶ *Parents sometimes need to make time to talk to their children about their feelings.*

Who gets bullied and why?

Anyone can become a victim of bullying but some people seem more likely to be bullied than others. A gang of bullies may pick on people who they see as different from themselves. For example, their victim might wear glasses, have a stutter, or be overweight. They might be from a different ethnic group or follow a different religion. They might come from a poorer family than those of the gang members, or they might be richer.

> "I used to pick on other kids who were going through a hard time. They would get upset so easily it made me feel better about all the things going on at home for me."
>
> Lisa, age 14

◀ Bullies will often target people who are having problems at home or with their schoolwork.

Gangs also bully vulnerable and unhappy children because they see them as an easy target. Children who do not feel good about themselves may even believe that they deserve the bullying.

Bullying affects people in different ways. Some children may feel able to deal with the bullying on their own and it stops. For them it will have been an unpleasant experience but may not have done any lasting harm. For others the effects can be very different. They do not feel able to handle the bullying and no matter what the victim tries to do it will not stop.

▲ *Victims of bullying can find it hard to trust other children and make friends.*

"I shall remember this for all eternity. Monday: my money is taken. Tuesday: names are called. Wednesday: my uniform is torn. Thursday: my body is pouring with blood. Friday: It's ended. Saturday: Freedom."

An entry in the diary of 13-year-old Vijay Singh, who committed suicide in 1996. His mother found his diary after his death.

Just watching…

When a gang is bullying people, there are often plenty of other people who know what is going on. They may even see bullying taking place but do nothing to stop it. What makes people behave in this way?

▲ Children sometimes admire a gang for being tough, instead of trying to stop their behavior.

Sometimes it is just easier to stand and watch than to get involved. People may feel afraid that if they try to stop the bullying, the gang will pick on them next. Or they might want to be accepted by the gang—even if that means supporting them when they bully. Some people get a kick out of watching someone else being bullied, even if they are not bullies themselves.

Katie didn't consider herself a bully; she'd been bullied in her primary school and now just kept her head down. When her best friend started being bullied by Natalie's gang she didn't know what to do. If she stood up to them she'd get bullied as well, but if she stood by and just watched she'd lose her friend. What would you do?

Standing by and doing nothing gives more power to the bullies. It makes the gang feel that no one dares stand up to them and encourages them to carry on. The victim feels even more alone.

When people see a gang of bullies at work, or know that bullying is taking place, they have several choices. They can stand up to the gang, to show them that they are not all-powerful. They can tell an adult. Or they may choose to walk away. Each of these options has a consequence. Remember, doing nothing gives power to the gang. Next time, the victim could be you.

▲ *It can be hard to decide how to deal with bullies. People sometimes prefer to push the problem to the back of their mind and hope the bullying stops.*

Dealing with bullying

When it comes to dealing with bullying it is important to remember the two Ts: Telling and Talking.

It is OK to tell about bullying. There is a feeling in some schools that telling is being babyish or disloyal. Telling about bullying is none of these things. Many people feel afraid to tell. Sometimes they feel the bullying will get worse. But if they don't tell, the gangs of bullies will carry on anyway, and there are almost certainly other people who are being picked on by them.

▼ *It takes courage to tell on a bully—victims often fear the problem will just get worse.*

That long road

Walking up that road to school I
    consider turning back
I consider running to that special
    point, my own special point.
I consider going to their houses
    and telling their moms.
I consider running their lives
    somehow—to make them feel
    scared.
Then suddenly I'm in school, they
    take my bag, ruffle my hair.
Maybe some other day.

Kate

Talking about what is happening can help people feel better. Many victims of bullying want to try to deal with it themselves and just need some ideas and support to tackle the problem. Talking to a school counselor, teacher, parent, or another trusted adult can help. Sticking with a group of friends can help, too—a group is more powerful than one person on his or her own, as the gang of bullies knows only too well.

Sometimes the bullies themselves want to stop bullying but don't know how. Bullying becomes part of who they are, part of their character, and they just do it out of habit. If they belong to a gang of bullies they may be under pressure from other gang members to keep bullying. Again, a school counselor or other trusted adult may be able to suggest how to break the bullying habit.

▼ *Telling a parent can be the first step to solving a bullying problem.*

6. Leaving a gang

Gangs for ever?

Most people only belong to a gang for a short period of time. There are as many different reasons for people leaving gangs as there are for joining.

We have seen that joining a gang can be a normal part of growing up. As people get older, they usually feel more confident and no longer need the security of being part of a gang. They might find that having one or two close friends is more important to them. Some gang members decide to leave a gang once they have children of their own to care for. They may no longer want to be involved in risky behavior such as crime or drug abuse.

▼ *Many people find that their interests change as they grow older. Activities such as sports give them the excitement they used to get from being in a gang.*

FACT:
Studies of gangs done since the 1920s have shown that most young people stay in a gang for no more than one year. Studies by Miller (1982) and Spergel (1991)

▲ *A Guardian Angel on patrol in Detroit, Michigan*

Others leave gangs when they move to a new area or change schools. The situation that led them to join a gang in the first place may no longer exist, so they do not feel they need to join another one. They have an opportunity to make new friends. When people get jobs, they may find they no longer have time for the gang, or they find that their interests change.

FACT:
The Guardian Angels were set up in New York in 1979 and are now found in many American cities. Guardian Angel groups are mostly made up of teenagers who have managed to break free from violent gangs. They patrol the streets, parks, and subway stations, trying to keep ordinary people safe from gang violence.

Making the break

Some people find it easy to leave a gang, but for others it is much more difficult. Gang members who have made a promise of loyalty may find it hard to break their promise. Other gang members may put pressure on them to stay. This kind of pressure might be especially strong in gangs such as the Mafia. Since families are often involved in these gangs, a member may be afraid that, if they leave, they will lose their families as well.

"Jumping out" is when a gang member suddenly decides to leave a street gang. Other gang members feel betrayed that anyone could dare to leave their gang, and they make it very difficult for that person to leave. They will let people go, but not before they have taught them a severe lesson by beating them up. These beatings are much worse than the ones given during an initiation rite.

▼ *This Mafia member in Sicily decided to give evidence about other gang members to the police. He needed close protection, in case the Mafia tried to kill him.*

An easier and safer way to leave a street gang is to "fade out." This means that you gradually stop hanging out with the gang, until there comes a time when you stop going out with them altogether.

▲ Parents, teachers, or counselors can suggest ways of breaking away from a gang.

Gang members who have been involved in serious crime sometimes ask for help from the police if they decide to leave. In exchange for protection, they give the police information about the gang's activities. They can also seek help from their own families and school counselors.

But for most young people, leaving a gang is not quite so dangerous. Talking to a trusted adult is a first step. Tackling problems such as drug addiction will reduce reliance on the gang. (There are some useful numbers at the back of this book.) Developing new interests and making new friends can also be a ways of making the break.

GLOSSARY

Addicts
People who use substances such as alcohol, cigarettes, or illegal drugs and feel sick if they do not use them regularly.

Anti-social behavior
Behavior that makes life unpleasant for people around you, but is not actually illegal.

Bribe
To promise someone money or other rewards in exchange for favors. For example, a police officer might be given money in return for agreeing not to arrest gang members.

Cartel
A group that controls the way particular goods (e.g., illegal drugs) are produced and sold.

Code of Ethics
Rules that set out how gang members should behave.

Crime syndicate
Several gangs working together to carry out crime.

Drive-by shooting
Shooting someone from a vehicle as it drives past.

Ethnic minority
A group whose language, skin color, religion, or traditions are different from most of the other people in a country.

Immigrants
People who have left one country to come and live in a different one.

Intimidate
To scare or threaten.

Joyriding
Driving a stolen car, often in a dangerous way.

Mafia
A secret criminal organization that began in Sicily. The word "mafia" is now often used to mean any large criminal organization.

Neo-Nazis
People who have very extreme political views, including the idea that white people are better than other people.

Pledge
A promise.

Racists
People who hate people from other cultures.

Rap
Songs in which the words are chanted or spoken to a beat. Gangsta rap music is often about violence or urban street life.

Rites
A series of rituals carried out for a particular purpose, for example, to mark someone's acceptance into a gang.

Ritual
An action that has to be carried out in a set way, often as part of a ceremony.

Substance abuse
Using substances such as alcohol or glue in a way that can damage your health.

Suicide
Killing yourself.

Tattoos
Pictures and symbols on the body made by injecting ink under the skin.

Vandalism
Destroying or damaging property.

FURTHER INFORMATION

ORGANIZATIONS

United States
Boys and Girls Clubs of America
1230 W. Peachtree Street, NW _
Atlanta, GA 30309
(404) 487-5700
http://www.bgca.org

G.R.E.A.T. (Gang Resistance
Education and Training)
Bureau of Alcohol, Tobacco, and
Firearms
(800) 726-7070
http://www.atf.treas.gov/great/i
ndex.htm#

Koch Crime Institute
700 SW Jackson, Ste. 400
Topeka, KS 66603
(785) 234-5624
http://www.kci.org

Great Britain
Anti-Bullying Campaign
10 Borough High Street
London SE1 9QQ
Helpline: 020 7378 1446
(9.30am- 5pm, Mon-Fri)

ChildLine
0800 1111
A free confidential 24-hour
helpline for children and young
people in trouble or danger

FURTHER READING

Ewing, Lynne. *Drive-By*.
Harpercollins Juvenile Books,
1998.

Goldentyer, Debra. *Street
Violence*. Raintree Steck-
Vaughn, 1998.

Salak, John. *Violent Crime: Is It
Out of Control?* Twenty-First
Century, 1995.

Schwartz, Michael. *Luis
Rodriguez*. Raintree Steck-
Vaughn, 1997.

Resources

*Do You Know a Safe Place?
What Every Person Should
Know About Youth Gangs*
by Vacker Cathey
(Bookpartners Inc)

*Gangs in School: Signs,
Symptoms and Solutions*
by Arnold P Goldstein
(Research PR Co)

*The Boys who Sat by the
Window: Helping Children Cope
with Violence* by Chris Loftis
(New Horizons)

INDEX